Three Years

Jade Van Jaarsveld

BookLeaf Publishing

Presentation by *BookLeaf Publishing*

Web: www.bookleafpub.com

E-mail: info@bookleafpub.com

ISBN: 9789357212496

First edition 2023

For Gran

ACKNOWLEDGEMENT

I would like to thank my family, not only for consistently putting up with me, but more specifically: my late Gran, who passed down her creativity and love of words, art and poems to me. My Mum who gave me an additional love of reading and has always been my eager, much-appreciated, honest critic. My Dad, for always cheering me on and also regularly reminding me of a quote from Norman Vincent Peale: 'Shoot for the moon. Even if you miss, you'll land among the stars.' My Brother for often being unknowingly able to pull me out of ruts. I love you all dearly.

I would definitely like to thank all my friends for being my keen and supportive listeners/readers and for all that they do to keep me sane – love you all.

Additionally, I would also like to thank all my English teachers throughout school for always having faith in me and encouraging me to keep writing.

Last but not least, I would like to thank BookLeaf Publishing for creating this opportunity.

PREFACE

This collection contains little pieces of me from over the last three years. My hope is that these fragments provide some comfort to readers in similar situations. They are not always happy and positive but then, neither is life. However, I am a strong believer in that, without the bad, it is much harder to appreciate the good.

The Forest Flees & A Tree Is Left Behind

I do not deal with change well.
Every silly little online quiz I lied on
When asked if I accept or reject change.

I said that I do not want to go to uni.
That was my choice. I must remember.
But I can't get rid of the feeling –

The feeling of being left behind.
Seasons will change, just like lives
And all my friends will say goodbye –

And I – by my own choice –
Will be left to my own devices
And a fear of having made the wrong choices.

I struggle to voice these fears of mine
In the fear that someone will react with
"But it was your choice to be left behind."

My choice, my choice, my choice –
Yes, it was. But I am allowed to fear
What will become of my future.

I am still allowed to wonder
What could have happened
If I had chosen the other path.

I am a tree. Rooted to the ground.
Unable to move from where I am stood.
Mud doesn't hide these roots –

Memories hide these roots.
Fears hide these roots.
Ambition hides these roots.

The forest of friends, of family,
Can let go of these memories, these fears
But my self-pitying tears

Water the ground I am rooted to.
Will I die if I move? From this fixed spot?
Will I thrive if I move? From this fixed spot?

Maybe I am just not ready yet.
Maybe these roots are not strong enough yet
To carry the weight that I am, alone.

I am a tree.
The rest of the forest flees, searching
For better water, better soil, better sun.

One day my roots will come undone –

Free from the memories, the fears,
Keeping them underground.

I just need to grow a little more.

Observation from the Conservatory

A big fat
Feathery pigeon
Shudders as it
Lands on the
Sweet orange
Fence.

The cat
Trills.

Magpies glide
And dart
Through clear sky;
Two for joy.
They land
On a tree
Opposite
My house.

The cat
Trills.

I have always liked
That tree. It's

Branches
Are always bare
When I pay
Attention to it.
I believe it has
Always stood
There naked.
One magpie
Departs.

The cat
Trills.

One for sorrow.
Or is it two again?
No. It is just that
Big black bin bag
That has seemingly
Been caught on that
Tree for an eternity.
Proof that when
Humans taint
The world, we taint
It for good.

Magpie leaves.
Cat leaves.

The bin bag
Never leaves.

Observation of Memory

I remember
The good times
Like
I remember
The bad times
And
The bad times
Like
The good times

Messily

Written on paper
Scrunched up
Thrown in a bin
But the bin throws
It back at me again

Or

Displayed on a
Pin board
Centre-piece
But I get so
Many more

That eventually
Other things
Cover it up

Or

Locked away in
Pandora's box
For safe
Keeping
Preserving the past
And protecting
The present me
Only
I know I will open
It one day again

Or

Impulsively

I recall a
Sharp
Fragment
And I grasp
It 'til my hand
Bleeds with the
Pain of the memory
Bleeds back into

The forefront
Of my brain
And I don’t
Let go until
The damage
Is done and I
Am left a mess

The fragment is
A plug in my hand
It stops the bleeding

But

It hurts to hold onto
And
It hurts to let go.

Observation of a Dead Leaf in Summer

Tumble-weeding
Down the lane

Do you ever wonder if
The dead leaves feel pain?

Tumble-weeding
Down the lane

Snap-crackle-pop
In the heat, slain

Tumble-weeding
Down the lane

Its frail body crunches,
Tip-tapping the terrain

Tumble-weeding
Down the lane

Man crisp-packet-cracks
Its body, sounds like pain

Remnants blow
Down the lane

Pieces settle
Nestling into
Rustling grass

Decomposing

Circle of life
Is sustained

Helped by
Others, pained

Observation of a Spider During a Thunderstorm

She stays in the corner
On the outside of my window.

Lighting flashes
Thunder booms
Rain pelts

She seems confused,
Rushes to the parts
Of her web that shake;
Finds no sustenance.

Lighting flashes
Thunder booms
Rain pelts

She is in an action movie now.
Her harness has broken,
She is spinning out of control
With each drop, provoked.
She twirls, whirls, spirals,
No amateur in acrobatics.

Lightning flashes
Thunder booms
Rain pelts

She falls.
Heart stops.
But she catches herself.
I don't like spiders,
I never did,
But I have to admit
I am fascinated
By her perseverance.

Lightning flashes
Thunder booms
Rain pelts

She has learnt her lesson,
Runs back to the corner of
The window for safety,
Shaken by the trauma
And yet stronger because of it.
I stand in awe of a creature
I fear out of classical conditioning;
I wish I had her perseverance.
/I can have her perseverance./
Nature can teach us a thing or two.

Lightning flashes
Thunder booms
Rain pelts

We just have to observe.

A Confession & An Affirmation

This is but one chapter of life
Yet I feel like a tourist in a foreign cathedral.
The one who is not there for the faith.

They admit it.
They are merely there for the
Sights of stunning stained glass
And fail to see the relevance of prayer.
They have no need for these
Spiritual conventions…

But without them, what am I?
A piece of meat, of steak,
Left untouched on a Friday
By the Christian family?

I am as much a part of
My Faith
As it is a part of me

And God is my ghost-writer.
I should trust his hand more
In my simple game of life.

Science or Religion?

Science or Religion?
A debate that irks many.

Do you wish to listen
About how many particles
Make you up?
About what mutation
Will occur if you forget
Important nucleic information?
About how we, as human beings,
Are only operational at
Certain temperatures?

Or would you prefer to
Listen to a Nun?
Let Sister Mary tell you
About how God
Hand-picked each of our
Features, tip-to-top,
Including our noses.

I believe they go hand-in-hand,
Science and religion.
You cannot stamp out either
From each other's argument.

If you only strongly believe in
One or the other
You shall forever remain
On /only/ the brink of realism.

Stillwater

/She sits. She stares. Her expression is deadpan./

I creep out
Say I am going
To the loo
But I sneak
To the front door
Grab my already
Packed backpack
Unlock the door
Go

/There is a voice in the background, sometimes fast, sometimes slow, but always grave, muffled by her distracted silence. She can never focus on it long./

I am going to be sick.
But just as fast as that
Pit builds with every
Step away from there
It also plateaus
The further away I am

The sun's warm touch
Assures me this is right

/She looks to the wall, to the floor, to the TV, out the window, down at the cat, plays with the frilly food mat on the table, switches the way she sits a ridiculous amount of times, plays with her hair, counts her toes, plays with her hair, pets the cat, looks at the other three who seem unnaturally able to concentrate, wonders why she is different, why this no longer works for her./

Nausea tiptoes around my stomach
Tickling the lining
Giggling at the
Wretched response
I am going to be sick
But why? Because I feel free?
Because I am getting closer
To being me?
That's the sad thing, don't you see?

/She is on autopilot. She is on autopilot every single time this happens. By now, she has learnt her script well. By now, she realises that the words will only ever be a script to her, that the words aren't ever going to be real to her. She always says them but never feels them. The words are always empty to her./

I don't walk for long.
There's a place I go
When I find it
When it calls to me
When I am drawn to it
Today I am drawn to it
Today I am drawn to the lake

/Sometimes she doesn't say the words. Sometimes she mouths them. Sometimes she pays attention to the other three and how they say the words with meaning when she never can. They speak with full, fat, heaving, meaningful, hopeful, passionate words; she speaks with hollow ones./

I am present by the lake
Painfully so
The ducks aren't out
So the water is still

The murky water
Is glass
Fragile
A mirror
Reflective
A mirror
In which I stare

At myself
In which I accuse
Myself
In which I scold
Myself
In which I beg
Myself
To just get on with it
To just get through it
But the answer is always
The same
"You must be still
You cannot disturb the surface"

My tears make ripples

/She cannot wait to get away. If she didn't care, she would just walk out. But that's the issue: she cares and loves too much, and she despises herself for it. Others always come before herself: like a reflex, an unstoppable automatic response, an irresistible reaction. She is never first. She tried that before but instead guilt claimed her, gripped her throat tight, suffocated her, stuck its fingers down her gullet and made her sick. Staying like this sickens her too though. Which is the lesser of two evils? Should she keep being selfless or should she finally be selfish?/

I cannot swim
I wonder if it would be quick
I wonder how long it would take
For the water to be still again
Once I'm gone
I'm too stubborn to go though
I'm not…done yet
So suffering in silence it is
Suffering in stillness
Suffering on a fence

/She could power an engine given how fast her leg is bobbing. She plays with her nails, she pulls at loose skin, she draws blood. She plays with her nails, plays with the cat, she gets glared at./

As I sit in the dirt
By the water
I realise
I am a stillwater stream
I had a beginning
I have an end to get to
But for now I am stagnant
The current in me is
Invisible or has died
I am simply hoping
The current is lost
For what is lost

Can be found
Just not right now

/It ends. She is relieved. She goes, hoping to find some peace after enduring an hour of heartache./

Whether I am
Stillwater or not
Something pours a vile
Of poisonous guilt
Into my waters
I go back
I go through it
Again
And
Again
And
Again…

/She has a week of relief./

I have an eternity of this
For as long as I am
Stillwater

Leaves

Learn to let go of people
Like a tree loses its leaves;
Sometimes you just need
To grow new ones.

A Letter to Me During Snowfall

24-01-2021

Dear Me,
Opposite your tiny conservatory stands a conifer. It is tall, dark and handsome - a strange sentiment to have for a tree but it is an evergreen. It's appearance never wilts, never changes (unless you account for the minute height growth it commits to annually) and always remains colourful.

The evergreen remains a beacon of hope during long, dark winters.

You like the evergreen.

You love evergreens in Winter.

Not only is it a symbol of hope, but also a symbol of perseverance.

In snowfall, the petite snowflakes gather on its branches and leaves, they gather until it is noticeable, until it is a new variation of beautiful.

Picturesque in summer, picturesque in winter is the evergreen.

But there is a tragedy that befalls it. When the white winter precipitation clusters, it clusters too much and doesn't realise the damage it will cause if fused together. The snow, once light when a single snowflake, joins together with more and becomes heavy, far too heavy for the branches of the evergreen.

It gets heavier.

And heavier.

Heavier still, until...

A crack.

The branch falters under the winter burden.

The bough breaks, clustered snowfall becomes white dust in the wind, a memory of what was once together; the broken branch lands on the twinkling ground below, lost and alone.

Not all is lost though.

The evergreen remains green, acknowledges it has more branches, continues, barely phased by its loss.

It knows the snow will not last forever.

It will fall, it will melt, it will return to how it was before like there was no such thing as snow before.

It will continue to live, to grow, accepting the experience as something that was intended to happen. It will remember the branch, for a tree never forgets, and it will prosper, the memory embedded in the grain of the wood, in the whisper of the wind that slowed its fall.

The experience inspired you to write a poem:

Winter Evergreen:

I am an evergreen in Winter
My branches hold up snowflakes
But when they cluster
When blizzards form
My branches break
For I cannot hold
The weight anymore

Make sure you take care of yourself, acknowledge stress and unpleasant times. Do not swipe them up under the carpet, ready to trip on and for it to come out in a mess.

Be more like the evergreen that prospers through good and bad.

Love,
Your Inner Poet

Spinning Top

/Black with colour on top/
/Don’t let it stop/
/Spin, spin, little spinning-top/

Faster than the eye can see –
What my eye can see is
The Earth ever turning
One side always yearning
For the day.

Orange marks the core –
I see the sunset, yellow,
Twilight shown by pink,
Purple.

Earth revolving.
People evolving.

And yet I stay the same.

/Black with colour on top/
/Don’t let it stop/
/Spin, spin, little spinning-top/

Bestie

The first thing I remember is that we
Used to sing karaoke in your
Monochromatic living room –
I hated your black leather couches
But I loved spending time with you.
You wanted to sing 'Hot'n'Cold' by Katy Perry alone;
I couldn't keep my big mouth shut long
Enough for your solo, always joining in
On 'you're yes and you're no'
"/No/, this is /my/ song," you would say, "let me sing it…"
It was /our/ song even though we fell out over it often.

I don't remember meeting you
We kinda just happened
Like our every-weekend-sleepovers
Like our midnight snack ritual of
Cheap Coke and Cheerios
(No milk, dry)
Like our friendship with the elderly binman
Who taught us to pick up the rubbish
In your area, bring it to him so
We could bin it and then be rewarded,

Not just with a cleaner environment but
With those sticky, sour, star sweets that
Always made me cringe with the
Fizzy tang on my taste buds.

We were inseparable
Like your connection with your
Bolt-the-dog teddy bear
Like my connection with my
Teddy of Tigger
Like your addiction to Dr Pepper –
Never saw you leave home without a bottle
(I still don't know how you like it)
Like my addiction to Diet Pepsi

I remember our nights out at the pub
At age seven! Down at the Lizzie
With your mum and step-dad,
"Heya Leslie, can we have two half-pints
Of Diet Coke?"
Remember that smell? Of soft, stale
Liquor and sweet cigarette smoke?
Remember the vibrating boom of the
Music, how we put our ears against
The cream walls, giggling as the sound
Waves tickled our earlobes?

I walk by your old house on the way back from work now,

Sometimes pause to look at the rickety fence,
Sometimes pause and whisper that's not the
front door I remember,
Sometimes pause and feel gross thinking about
how that's not your house anymore,
Sometimes pause and wonder if the new resident
sings karaoke in your living room.
Sometimes pause and wish I could go back to
simpler times.

Birds

Brutal cacophony
Of screams,
Bomb-siren-shrieking,
Heart beating
What's wrong?
What has disturbed you
Today, little, wingéd-friends?
What hair-raising issue
Has gathered you together
High above the trees today?
A princess's companion
You all are not.
Why do you screech
Incoherent speech
At each other?
What happened to
Sweet birdsong,
Morning hum,
Soft whistle?
Do you sense a threat?
Dear creatures, please,
Be calm for
Your caterwauling
Unnerves me.

Observation of Benches

There used to be
So many people
In Church.

All the rows would
Almost be filled
With life.

Now there are gaps
Like the gaps in
A mouth.

Where the tooth no
Longer grows.
The rows

Are emptier now.

I wonder if the wood
Remembers? If it
Senses it is

Missing a missing person
Passed onto the next
Life hereafter?

Does the grain feel the
Rain of quiet tears
Falling on it?

They will water it but
The bench will
Not bloom

Into a lost loved one. The
Memory of them
Lingers still.

Ghosts of the past sit with
Us in ceremony, souls
Lingering still.

Does the wood remember them?

INT. Bedroom II

Pillow says:
"Lie your head down."

Bed says:
"I will hold you up off the ground."

Duvet says:
"I will give you warm hugs."

I say:
That I will never leave.

Anxiety, on this day,
Acting in full fashion
As a blessing and curse,
Sits by my bedside,
Coos at me softly,
Offers me a hand,
Tuts when I refuse,
Insists we must leave.

Somehow

I leave
Later than intended.

I say:
"I will come back."

Pillow, Bed and Duvet nod
Silently say
"We will wait for you."

Daffodils

Amongst the black and white
They bring flavour to my room,
Small and yellow and bright.

They reach toward the light;
No matter how dark it is,
They fight through their plight.

Thank you, Grandmother,
We have grown apart but
You gave them to me, not another.

You told me that they were for
Me. I said I was unwell and so
You bought daffodils. You were sure

That they would add colour
To my room. They did.
Bad thoughts they blur.

Remind me, Daffodils:

/You must reach towards the light;/
/No matter how dark it is,/
/You must fight through your plight./

Gaps

I would smile
But I am
Missing teeth.

/The benches/
/Aren't as full as/
/I remember/

There is chatter
Quiet, cold, but
My mouth is shut.

/There is a space there/
/And a space there/
/And a – where did they/
/Sit again? There?/

I run my tongue
Over the smooth
Bloody gum.

/How does life keep/
/Going without them?/
/The gaps weren't always/
/There. They never were./

I picture the metallic
Liquid spread across
My tastebuds – bile builds.

/Something is missing./
/Someone is missing./
/This emptiness is unnatural./

The gaps are unnatural.
The taste, nauseating.
The smoothness, wrong.

/But this is what happens/
/When you grow up,/
/When you get used to a place,/
/When you get used to a people./

It is the wrong kind of smooth.
Slimy, sickening, painful,
It will likely heal
But not quick enough.

This is what happens
When you grow up.

Deflecting With Humour

"Why do you think you
Use humour to deflect?"

It hurts less to laugh
And even when it does
Hurt

When my lungs ache
For air because they have
Contracted so much,
When my stomach aches
Because the muscles have
Spasmed so much,
When the tears spring
From out of my eyes
Because my body doesn't
Know how else to
Express my amusement

It will always be a
More tolerable
More enjoyable
More desirable
Pain

Death Is...

An Autumn leaf's
Bone-crunching crack
Under foot
Jarring

A single feather
Drifting alone
In the breeze
Across paths
Walked by many
Ignored

The prolonged boiling
Of limescale water
In a white kettle –
Wait for the click

The tide releasing the shore

The tears of strangers
Who don't know why
They are mourning

Confusing

The sheer panic
Of stumbling your way
Into your lounge
In the pitch black
Only to realise
That the table
You knew was
Always
There
Is gone

Absence

Footprints in the snow
Covered with
Snow upon snow
Until you forget that
They were ever there

Cruel

A feeling known by
No other
Unspeakable
Recorded in a diary
Typed into a chatroom
Mouthed to your walls
Thought upon in the quiet

Ever-present on your lips
But you just can’t pronounce it

A distant memory
But still there

…

Oh, let me go and ask…

No. I can't…

Dying for something
Warm – oh, you know,
We haven't had
Apple Pie in a while!
Maybe she can make…

No. She can't…

Oh no! My trousers
Are too long – but
Gran can shorten…

No. She can't…

This would be perfect
For Gran, don't you
Think, Mum? But…

No. I can't get it…

Stuck outside again!

No key, dead phone
But, oh, I know –
I can knock and she'll…

No. She's not there anymore…

It Took a Death to Make Her a Hugger

It took a death to make her a hugger.
Her tears needed a solid shoulder
To land on. Her tears had to water
The renewing connection between
Her father, her brother, her mother.

Before, of any menial affection, she was a butcher,
For at the first sight of any hug, her cheeks would lose colour,
She would recoil, hiss like a snake, suffer,
When arms were placed around her body:
"You weren't like this when you were younger…"

When it happened, come later October,
The suddenness, the unexpectedness, stung her.
She thought they had all the time in the world, but, rather,
It had been five wordless months.
The earth took them back early winter.

It took a death to make her rediscover
The warmth she had missed when faced with a hugger:
A warmth that ceased the hunger
For affection,
A warmth that actually made her tougher.

It took a death to make her a lover
Of 'the dreaded embrace'.
Something that helped her to
Inevitably recover.

She just wished she had learnt it sooner.

www.ingramcontent.com/pod-product-compliance
Lightning Source LLC
Chambersburg PA
CBHW051738130826
49812CB00033B/910
9789357212496